The Great Lakes

Janet Piehl

Lerner Publications Company
Minneapolis

For Bridget
and Barrett

Lerner Publications Company
A division of Lerner Publishing Group, Inc.
241 First Avenue North
Minneapolis, MN 55401 U.S.A.

Website address: www.lernerbooks.com

Library of Congress Cataloging-in-Publication Data

Piehl, Janet.
    The Great Lakes / Janet Piehl.
        p.   cm. — (Lightning bolt books™—Famous places)
    Includes index.
    ISBN 978-0-7613-4456-8 (lib. bdg. : alk. paper)
    1. Great Lakes (North America)—Juvenile literature. I. Title.
    F551.P54 2010
    977—dc22   2009020000

Manufactured in the United States of America
1 — BP — 12/15/09

Contents

Welcome to the Great Lakes — page 5

Which Lakes Are Great Lakes? — page 9

How Did the Great Lakes Form? — page 14

Lake Life — page 17

Cleaning up the Lakes — page 25

Map — page 28

Fun Facts — page 29

Glossary — page 30

Further Reading — page 31

Index — page 32

Lake Superior

All five Great Lakes can be seen in this photo taken from space.

Lake Michigan

Welcome to the Great Lakes

What makes the Great Lakes great? Their size makes them great. The Great Lakes are a group of five huge lakes.

Lake Huron

Lake Ontario

Lake Erie

The Great Lakes are on the border of Canada and the north central United States.

Duluth, Minnesota, is in the Great Lakes region. Duluth is in the north central United States.

The Great Lakes are freshwater
lakes. This means they don't
contain salt water.

Freshwater lakes are
great for swimming
and kayaking.

The Great Lakes are all connected to one another. Rivers, smaller lakes, and canals join the lakes. The Great Lakes form the world's largest group of freshwater lakes.

A ship enters a canal that connects two Great Lakes.

Which Lakes Are Great Lakes?

Lake Superior is a Great Lake. It is the biggest, deepest, and coldest of the lakes. It is also farther north and west than the other lakes.

Split Rock Lighthouse in Minnesota sits on the northern shore of Lake Superior.

Lake Huron is another Great Lake. It is the second-biggest Great Lake. Lake Huron has a large bay. A bay is a section of a lake that is partly surrounded by land.

The blue waters of Georgian Bay lap the coast of Lake Huron.

Lake Huron and Lake Michigan meet at the Straits of Mackinac. The Straits of Mackinac is a narrow strip of water that connects the two lakes.

The Mackinac Bridge allows cars to cross the Straits of Mackinac.

Lake Erie is the shallowest Great Lake. It is also the warmest. New York, Ohio, Michigan, and Pennsylvania border Lake Erie.

A sunset over Lake Erie turns the sky pink, purple, and orange.

Lake Ontario is the smallest Great Lake. It is the farthest east as well. Water from Lake Ontario flows into the Saint Lawrence River. This river goes all the way to the Atlantic Ocean.

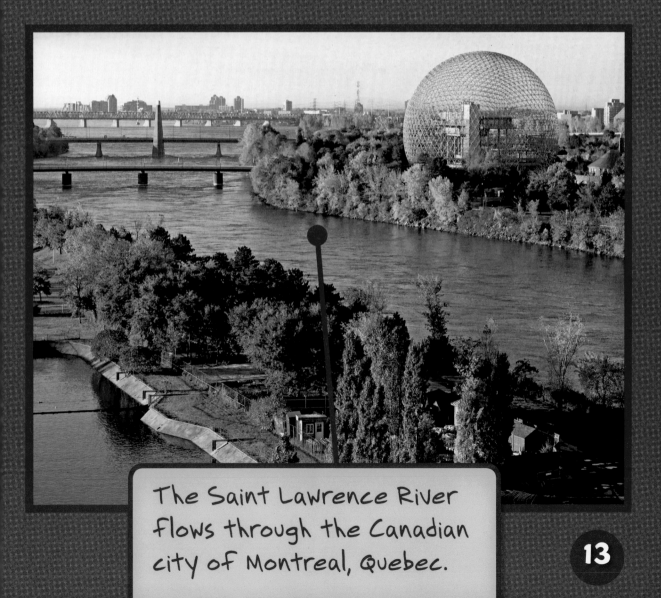

The Saint Lawrence River flows through the Canadian city of Montreal, Quebec.

How Did the Great Lakes Form?

The Great Lakes began forming millions of years ago. Huge moving sheets of ice called glaciers covered much of North America then.

The glaciers carried away dirt and large rocks. They scooped out huge holes in the ground. Over time, the glaciers melted. Water from the glaciers filled the holes.

The holes became the Great Lakes.

Glaciers such as this one helped form the Great Lakes.

15

Sand dunes meet the water on the coast of Lake Michigan.

Lake Life

Forests, wetlands, and sand dunes surround the Great Lakes. Cities also line the shores in some places.

The city of Chicago, Illinois, sits on the shore of Lake Michigan.

Many animals
live around the
Great Lakes.
Black bears,
deer, and
foxes are
among
these.

Black bears live
in the forests
near the Great
Lakes.

Some animals live right in the lakes!
Fish such as walleye, perch, and whitefish swim there.

Yellow perch can be found in all five of the Great Lakes.

People also call the Great Lakes area home. People have lived near the lakes for many years. Native Americans lived there as many as ten thousand years ago.

Some Native American groups that lived near the Great Lakes used birchbark canoes for water travel.

Native Americans took water and fish from the lakes. They hunted animals that lived nearby.

Native Americans canoe in Lake Superior.

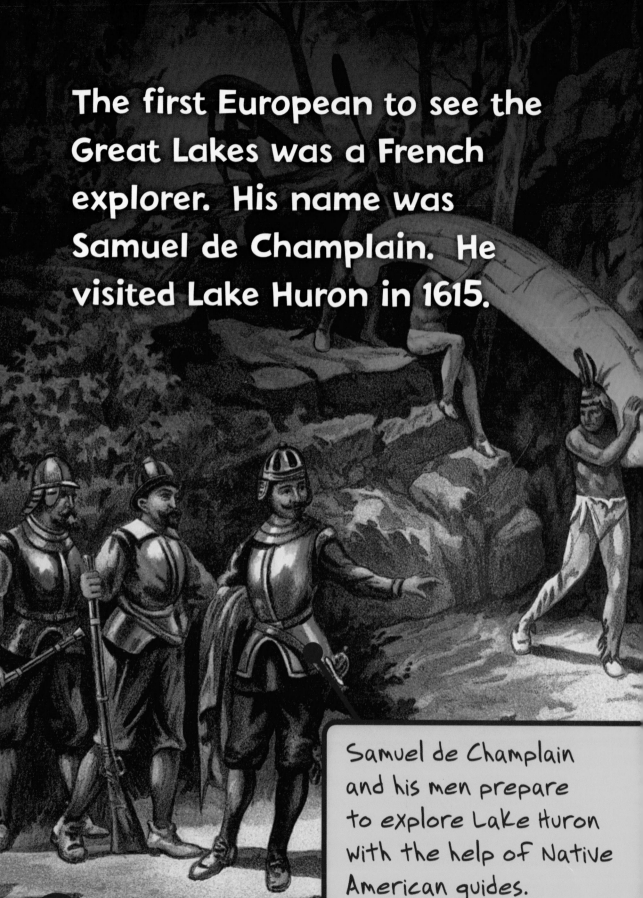

The first European to see the Great Lakes was a French explorer. His name was Samuel de Champlain. He visited Lake Huron in 1615.

Samuel de Champlain and his men prepare to explore Lake Huron with the help of Native American guides.

Soon more Europeans came to the Great Lakes. They also fished and hunted near the lakes. They built cities, farms, and factories there as well. Ships carried goods and people around the lakes.

This historical drawing shows Chicago in 1892.

Waste from a paper company drains into Lake Erie in this photo taken in 1968.

People began dumping garbage and factory waste into the lakes. By the 1960s, the lakes were very polluted.

Cleaning up the Lakes

The United States and Canada worked together to clean up the lakes. They made laws to limit what people could dump into the lakes. The lakes' waters are healthier. But we must still work to keep the Great Lakes clean.

People clean up an oil spill near the shores of Lake Erie.

The Great Lakes are very important.

Millions of people drink water that comes from the lakes. People also depend on goods from ships that sail the lakes.

A ship sails through chunks of winter ice on Lake Huron.

People enjoy the Great Lakes too. They visit beaches, forests, and wetlands. They swim, sail, and fish. They enjoy the things that make the Great Lakes great.

Great Lakes Area

MINNESOTA

CANADA

Lake
Superior

MICHIGAN

Lake
Huron

Lake
Ontario

WISCONSIN

N

MICHIGAN

Lake
Erie

NEW
YORK

Lake
Michigan

ILLINOIS

INDIANA

OHIO

PENNSYLVANIA

| 0 | 40 | 80 Miles |
| 0 | 40 80 | 120 Kilometers |

CANADA

UNITED STATES

Great
Lakes

PACIFIC OCEAN

ATLANTIC OCEAN

MEXICO

Great
Lakes

UNITED
STATES

Fun Facts

- One way to remember the names of the Great Lakes is to think of the word **HOMES**. The letters stand for the first letter of each of the Great Lakes: Huron, Ontario, Michigan, Erie, and Superior.

- Lake Huron has about thirty thousand islands. Manitoulin Island is one of them. It is the world's largest island in freshwater.

- The Great Lakes do not usually freeze in winter. Only Lake Erie, the shallowest Great Lake, often freezes all the way across.

- Lake Superior is so big that it holds more water than all the other Great Lakes combined. It is one of the largest lakes in the world.

- The Great Lakes area is home to millions of people. One in four Canadians lives near the Great Lakes. One in ten people in the United States lives near the Great Lakes.

Glossary

bay: a section of a lake that is partly surrounded by land

canal: a waterway built by people. Canals connect bodies of water so that boats can travel between them.

dune: a large hill made when water and wind move sand into piles

freshwater: a word to describe a body of water that does not contain salt

glacier: a large sheet of ice that moves over land

polluted: very dirty. Water and land become polluted when people dump garbage on them.

wetland: land where the ground is wet. Marshes and swamps are wetlands.

Further Reading

Environmental Protection Agency Great Lakes National Program Office: Visualizing the Great Lakes
http://www.epa.gov/glnpo/image/index.htm

Great Lakes Kids
http://www.on.ec.gc.ca/greatlakes/For_Kids-WS4DB7BBAD-1_En.htm

Johnson, Rebecca L. *A Journey into a Lake.* Minneapolis: Lerner Publications Company, 2004.

Valzania, Kimberly. *Great Lakes.* New York: Children's Press, 2004.

Walker, Sally M. *Glaciers.* Minneapolis: Lerner Publications Company, 2008.

Index

bay, 10

Canada, 6, 25
canals, 8

deer, 18

freshwater, 7–8, 29

glaciers, 14–15

Lake Erie, 5, 12, 24–25, 29

Lake Huron, 5, 10–11, 22, 26, 29

Lake Michigan, 4, 11, 16–17, 29
Lake Ontario, 5, 13, 29
Lake Superior, 4, 9, 21, 29

Native Americans, 20–22

Saint Lawrence River, 13
Samuel de Champlain, 22
sand dunes, 16–17
Straits of Mackinac, 11

United States, 6, 25, 29

Photo Acknowledgments

The images in this book are used with the permission of: © Stocktrek Images/Getty Images, pp. 4–5; © Panoramic Images/Getty Images, p. 6; © Henry Georgi/All Canada Photos/Getty Images, pp. 7, 27; © age fotostock/SuperStock, pp. 8, 26, 31; © Gene Ahrens/SuperStock, p. 9; © Andre Gallant/Riser/Getty Images, p. 10; © Bill Barley/SuperStock, p. 11; © altrendo nature/Altrendo/Getty Images, p. 12; © Philippe Renault/hemis.fr/Getty Images, p. 13; © Robert Harding Picture Library/SuperStock, pp. 14–15; © Bullaty-Lomeo/The Image Bank/Getty Images, p. 16; © Hisham Ibrahim/Photodisc/Getty Images, p. 17; © James Hager/Robert Harding World Imagery/Getty Images, p. 18; © Kevin Cullimore/Dorling Kindersley/Getty Images, p. 19; Lakeshore Museum Center, p. 20; Charles Lanman, Minnesota Historical Society, p. 21; © Bridgeman Art Library, London/SuperStock, p. 22; Library of Congress, p. 23 (LC-DIG-pga-00664); © Alfred Eisenstaedt/Time & Life Pictures/Getty Images, p. 24; AP Photo/Carlos Osorio, p. 25; © Laura Westlund/Independent Picture Service, p. 28; © Ethan Meleg/All Canada Photos/Getty Images, p. 30.

Front Cover: © Terry Donnelly/The Image Bank/Getty Images.